FEELING DISAPPOINTED

by Joy Berry • Illustrated by Maggie Smith

SCHOLASTIC INC.

New York Toronto London Auckland Sydney
Mexico City New Delhi Hong Kong Buenos Aires

ISBN 0-439-34159-0

10 9 8 7 6 5 4 3 2 1   02 03 04 05 06
Printed in the U.S.A.
First printing, April 2002

Hello, my name is Cosmo.

I live with Patrick.

Sometimes people say they'll do something for Patrick, but then they don't.

Patrick feels disappointed.

Sometimes things don't happen the way
Patrick wants them to happen.

Patrick feels disappointed.

When you feel disappointed,
you feel let down.

Disappointment can make you feel angry, frustrated, discouraged, or distrustful.

Feeling disappointed is no fun.

You might get angry with a person who has disappointed you.

You might wonder if that person is going to let you down the next time.

Disappointment can cause you to worry.

You might worry that things won't
work out the way you want them to.

When you're disappointed, you can
do things to make yourself feel better.

First, admit that you're upset.

If someone has disappointed you, let the person know how you feel.

Then give the person a chance to explain what happened.

Try to be understanding.

When someone offers an apology,
accept it.

Try not to say mean things to a person who has disappointed you.

Saying mean things will only make the situation worse.

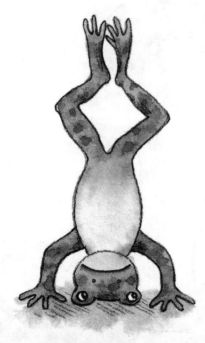

Try not to let the same people disappoint you.

If a situation continues to disappoint you, plan to do something else.

Try not to waste time and energy hoping for things that won't happen.

Try not to let disappointment with one friend ruin your relationships with other friends.

Remember that people usually keep their promises.

Try new things.

Don't think that everything will go wrong just because one situation didn't work out.

Everyone feels disappointed once in a while.

Feeling disappointed is normal.

Just try to do things to make yourself feel better whenever you feel disappointed.

Let's talk about ... **Joy Berry!**

As the inventor of self-help books for kids, Joy Berry has written over 250 books that teach children about taking responsibility for themselves and their actions. With sales of over 80 million copies, Joy's books have helped millions of parents and their kids.

Through interesting stories that kids can relate to, Joy Berry's Let's Talk About books explain how to handle even the toughest situations and emotions. Written in a clear, simple style and illustrated with bright, humorous pictures, the Let's Talk About books are fun, informative, and they really work!